Copycat Recipes

Second Edition

A step by step cookbook
to prepare your
favorite restaurants' dishes: delicious meat dishes,
special dressing,
and many new dinner recipes

Linda Smith

Introduction

You have the opportunity to increase your culinary knowledgeby following the recipes in this book.

If you want to surprise your relatives and friends with a fantastic dinner, by reading this cookbook you will find many tasty meat recipes and various secrets about seasonings to putin the dishes.

You will be followed step by step on each recipe, with thepossibility to change each ingredient to your liking.

You will see that your diners will not be disappointed by yourdishes and will definitely want to come back and taste your delicious recipes. These copycat recipes have been tested repeatedly to make sure that you are creating authentic dishes from the most famous restaurants. Expert cooks spend hours tweaking thoserecipes to get the taste just right. These recipes are as near thereal thing as sitting your favorite restaurant proper in your kitchen.

You do not leave the house, do not wait in line, and do not waste money on luxurious food, just the mouth-watering tasteof your favorite restaurant meals and the guarantee that you can recreate them in your kitchen whenever you want. Come to think of the money you can save and all the time lost waiting in line. Using the simple copycat recipes from the mostfamous restaurants, you can create your favorite restaurant dishes at home!

Very soon, right before your eyes, you can now start cookinglike a high-end restaurant chef and save most of your time! Another relevant advantage of these recipes is that you can twist some ingredients that suit your tastes

Chapter 1

Dinner Recipes

P.F. Chang's Beef and Broccoli

Preparation Time: 45 minutes

Cooking Time: 15 minutes

Servings: 4

Ingredients

- Marinade:

- 1/3 cup oyster sauce

- 2 teaspoons toasted sesame oil

- 1/3 cup sherry

- 1 teaspoon soy sauce

- 1 teaspoon white sugar

- 1 teaspoon corn starch

- Beef and Broccoli:

- ¾ pound beef round steak

- 3 tablespoons vegetable oil

- 1 thin slice of fresh ginger root

- 1 clove garlic, peeled and smashed

- 1-pound broccoli, cut into florets

Directions:

1. Incorporate marinade ingredients in a bowl until they have dissolved. Marinate the beef in the mixture for 30 minutes. Sauté the ginger and garlic in hot oil for a minute. When the oil is flavored, remove the garlic and ginger and add in the broccoli. Continue cooking the broccoli until tender.

2. Once cooked, situate it to a bowl and set aside. Pour the beef and the marinade into the pan in which you cookedthe broccoli and continue cooking until beef is cooked, or about 5 minutes. Pour the broccoli back in and keep cooking for another 3 minutes. Serve.

Nutrition:

331 Calories

21.1g Fat

21.7g Protein

Outback's Secret Seasoning Mix for Steaks

Preparation Time: 5 minutes

Cooking Time: 10 minutes

Servings: 3

Ingredients

Seasoning:

- 4–6 teaspoons salt

- 4 teaspoons paprika

- 2 teaspoons ground black pepper

- 1 teaspoon onion powder

- 1 teaspoon garlic powder

- 1 teaspoon cayenne pepper

- ½ teaspoon coriander

- ½ teaspoon turmeric

Directions:

1. Blend all the seasoning ingredients in a bowl. Rub the spice blend into the meat on all sides and let rest for 15-20 minutes before cooking.

Nutrition

16.4 Calories

0.5g Total Fat

3.5g Carbohydrates

Taco Bell's Chalupa

Preparation Time: 40 minutes

Cooking Time: 10 minutes

Servings: 8

Ingredients

Tortillas:

- 2½ cups flour

- 1 tablespoon baking powder

- ½ teaspoon salt

- 1 tablespoon vegetable shortening

- 1 cup milk

- Oil, for deep frying

- Filling:

- 1 tablespoon dried onion flakes

- ½ cup water

- 1-pound ground beef

- ¼ cup flour

- 1 tablespoon chili powder

- 1 teaspoon paprika

- 1 teaspoon salt

- Some oil for frying

- For Garnishing:

- Some sour cream

- Some lettuce, shredded

- Some cheddar cheese or Monterey Jack cheese

- Some tomato, diced

Directions:

2. Combine the flour, baking powder, and salt. Stir in the vegetable shortening and mix. Then add the milk and continue mixing. Portion the dough into 8 parts, and then shape them into 8 6-inch tortillas.

3. Deep fry the tortillas until golden brown. Set aside to cool. Start making the filling. Place the onion flakes in the water and set aside for 5 minutes. Mix the rest of the filling ingredients (except the oil) together until combined. Add in the onion with the water and continue mixing. Heat the oil in a skillet, and then cook the entire beef mixture until the beef browns.

4. Now, assemble your Chalupas. In the tortillas, place the following by layers:

5. Cooked beef mixture; Sour cream; Lettuce; Cheese; and lastly Tomatoes.

6. Serve on a plate.

Nutrition

424.9 Calories

15.8g Total Fat

21.6g Protein

Chili's Baby Back Ribs

Preparation Time: 15 minutes

Cooking Time: 3 hours 30 minutes

Servings: 4

Ingredients

- Pork:

- 4 racks baby-back pork ribs

- Sauce:

- 1½ cups water

- 1 cup white vinegar

- ½ cup tomato paste

- 1 tablespoon yellow mustard

- 2/3 cup dark brown sugar packed

- 1 teaspoon hickory flavored liquid smoke

- 1½ teaspoons salt

- ½ teaspoon onion powder

- ¼ teaspoon garlic powder

- ¼ teaspoon paprika

Directions:

1. Combine all of the sauce ingredients and then bring to a boil. Let it simmer for 45 to 60 minutes, stir it occasionally. When it's done, preheat oven at 300 degrees. Cover the 1 rack of ribs with aluminum foil. Putthe ribs on top.

2. Take out the sauce from heat and start glazing over the ribs.

3. When it is completely covered, and transfer it on the baking pan with the foil opening facing upwards. Do it again for the remaining racks and bake it for 2½ hours. When it is almost done, prepare your grill at medium heat then cook both sides. Brush some more sauce on each side and grill for another minutes. Don't overcook. Once done, serve with extra sauce.

Nutrition:

645 Calories

43.8g Total Fat

51.5g Protein

Cracker Barrel's Green Beans with Bacon

Preparation Time: 10 minutes

Cooking Time: 45 minutes

Servings: 6

Ingredients

- ¼ pound sliced bacon, cut into 1-inch pieces

- 3 cans (14.5 ounces each) green beans, with liquid

- ¼ yellow onion, peeled, chopped

- 1 teaspoon granulated sugar

- ½ teaspoon salt

- ½ teaspoon fresh ground black pepper

Directions:

1. Half-cook the bacon in a saucepan—make sure it does not get crispy. Add the green beans with the liquid to the browned bacon and season with salt, pepper, and sugar. Top the green beans with the onion and then cover the pan until the mixture boils. Decrease the heat and let mixture to simmer for another 45 minutes before serving.

Nutrition:

155.3 Calories

9g Total Fat

6g Protein

P.F. Chang's Spare Ribs

Preparation Time: 5 minutes

Cooking Time: 25 minutes

Servings: 2

Ingredients

- Sauce:

- 1 cup ketchup

- 1 cup light corn syrup

- ½ cup hoisin sauce

- ½ cup water

- 1/3 cup light brown sugar, packed

- 2 tablespoons onions, minced

- 1 tablespoon rice vinegar

- Ribs:

- 12 to 16 cups water

- 2 teaspoons salt

- 1 rack pork spareribs

- 4 cups vegetable oil

- 1 teaspoon sesame seeds, for garnish

- 1 tablespoon green onion, diced, for garnish

Directions:

1. Stir in all of the sauce ingredients and wait it to boil then let it simmer for 5 minutes. Set aside. Transfer the water and salt into a large pot then let it boil. In the meantime, clean the spare ribs and take out the excess fat.

2. When it starts to boil, transfer all the ribs into the water and continue boiling for 14 minutes. Drain and set aside. Cook the oil at 375 degrees then put 4 to 6 ribs in it and cook for 6 minutes.

3. Do it again until all the ribs are fried. Combine the fried ribs and the sauce over medium heat. Let it simmer at least a minute. Place the ribs to a plate and serve with rice. Topped the ribs with the sesame seeds and green onions.

Nutrition:

1344 Calories

77.2g Total Fat

52.5g Protein

Bonefish Grill Copycat Bang-Bang Shrimp

Preparation Time: 10 minutes

Cooking Time: 35 minutes

Serving: 10

Ingredients:

- 1 1/4 cups of mayonnaise, low fat

- 5/8 cup of chili sauce, Thai sweet

- 7 1/2 dashes of garlic-chili sauce

- 2 1/2 lbs. of shrimp, peeled

- 1/2 cup of corn starch

- 4 leaves of lettuce

- 1/4 cup of green onion, chopped

Directions:

1. Pour in sweet chili sauce and mayo together in large sized bowl. Add garlic-chili sauce. Stir well. Spread the corn starch into wide, shallow dish. Press the shrimp into corn starch, giving it a fairly thin layer of coating. Heat oil in deep-fryer to 350F.

2. Deep-fry the shrimp in small batches till not transparent in middle anymore, five minutes or so per

batch. Drain on plate lined with paper towels. Combine shrimp and mayo sauce in sauce bowl. Stir, coating shrimp well.

3. Line medium bowl using leaves of lettuce. Add shrimp to bowl. Garnish with the green onions. Serve.

Nutrition:

400 Calories

28g Total Fat

23g Protein

Black Angus Steakhouse's BBQ Baby Back Ribs

Preparation Time: 30 minutes

Cooking Time: 6 to 8 hours

Servings: 1

Ingredients

- 1 rack of pork ribs

- Your favorite barbecue sauces

- Onion powder, to taste

- Garlic powder, to taste

- Marinade:

- 2 tablespoons kosher salt

- 2 tablespoons paprika

- 4 tablespoons granulated garlic

- 1 tablespoon onion powder

- 1 teaspoon cumin seeds

- 1 teaspoon Durfee Ancho pepper

- 2 teaspoons dry mustard

- 2 teaspoons black pepper

- Rib Mop:

- 1 cup red wine vinegar

- 1 tablespoon garlic

- 1 cup water

- 3 tablespoons soy sauce

Directions:

1. Mix all of the marinade ingredients together. Rub the marinade all over the ribs to soak them in flavor.

2. Barbecue the meat over indirect heat at 250F to 300F for 3 to 4 hours. Add soaked fruit wood to the coals for additional aroma. Make sure that the temperature remains at 250F to 300F for the entire cookingduration. While the meat is cooking, mix together the rib mop ingredients in a bowl.

3. After three to four hours, transfer the meat to an aluminum pan and brush both sides with the rib mop.

4. Cook the ribs for another hour and then remove them from heat and mop them again. Continue cooking the ribs for another 3 to 4 hours, basting them with the mop and some barbecue sauce every hour. When the ribs are done barbecuing, sprinkle them with onion and garlic powder before

wrapping them in aluminum foil. Let the ribs rest for 30 minutes.

5. Situate the ribs to a plate and serve.

Nutrition

1500 Calories

30g Total Fat

14g Protein

Texas Road House's Mesquite Grilled Pork Chops with Cinnamon Apples

Preparation Time: 40 minutes

Cooking Time: 40 minutes

Serving: 2

Ingredients

- Cinnamon Apples:

- 4 apples (peeled, sliced)

- 2 tablespoons butter, melted

- 1/3 cup brown sugar

- 2 tablespoons lemon juice

- ¾ teaspoon cinnamon

- Pork Chop:

- 2 pork loin chops with bone, room temperature; 2inches thick

- Paste:

- 2 tablespoons extra virgin olive oil

- 2 tablespoons Worcestershire sauce

- 2 teaspoons black pepper, cracked

- 2 teaspoons chili powder

- 2 teaspoons granulated garlic powder

- 2 teaspoons kosher salt

- 1 teaspoon cumin, ground

- ½ teaspoon cinnamon, ground

- Mesquite wood chips, drenched in water for at least 30 minutes

Directions:

1. Prepare the apples by cooking all the cinnamon apple ingredients in butter until the apples soften. When they are ready, set the cooked apples aside. Reheat before serving.

2. Before you begin with the meat, you need to:

3. Soak the mesquite chips as instructed; leave the pork loin at room temperature for 30 to 45 minutes; and preheat the grill on high.

4. Thoroughly mix all the paste ingredients together. When the paste is done, spread it over the pork chops, covering them completely. Take out chips from the water and place them in an aluminum foil pan.

5. Place the pan directly over the fire from the grill and cook the pork loin on both sides for about 6 minutes. Once seared, set the heat to medium. Place the pork

over indirect medium heat and cook for another 25 minutes. Remove the pork from heat, wrap it in aluminum foil, and let rest for another 5 minutes. Transfer the pork to a plate with the reheated apples. Serve the entire dish.

Nutrition

Calories 22.5g

Total Fat 20

5g Protein

Panda Express's Grilled Teriyaki Chicken

Preparation Time: 5 minutes

Cooking Time: 20 minutes

Servings: 4

Ingredients

- 2 pounds chicken thighs

- 2 tablespoons canola oil

- 2/3 cup sugar

- ¼ cup low-sodium soy sauce

- 1 teaspoon lemon juice

- ½ teaspoon garlic powder

- ¼ teaspoon ground ginger

- 1/3 cup water

- 2 tablespoons cornstarch dissolved with 2 tablespoons water

- Sliced green onions for garnish

Directions

1. Incorporate chicken thighs and canola oil and let sit until the grill is hot. Situate the chicken in a grill pan

and grill for about 5 minutes on each side.

2. In a mixing bowl, combine the sugar, soy sauce, lemon juice, garlic powder, ground ginger and water. Heat to boiling, then decrease heat and simmer for 3 minutes. Stir in the cornstarch slurry and cook on low heat until the sauce thickens.

3. Spoon sauce over grilled chicken to serve. Sprinkle withsliced green onions.

Nutrition

452 Calories

10g Carbs

23g Protein

Panda Express's Sweet Fire Chicken Breast

Preparation Time: 15 minutes

Cooking Time: 15 minutes

Servings: 4

Ingredients

- 3 large chicken breasts, cut into 1-inch pieces

- 1 (10-ounce) bottle sweet chili sauce

- 1 medium onion, sliced

- 1 large red bell pepper, chopped

- 1¼ cup pineapple chunks

- ¼ cup pineapple juice

- 2 cloves garlic, minced

- 1 cup all-purpose flour

- 2 eggs, beaten

- Oil for frying

- 2 tablespoons oil, if needed

- Salt and pepper to taste

Directions

1. Incorporate flour, salt and pepper to a shallow dish. Dip the chicken pieces in the beaten egg followed by a dip in the flour to coat. Set aside.

2. Cook oil in a large skillet over medium-high heat. When hot, add the chicken pieces and cook until golden brown on all sides, about 6 minutes.

3. Once done, pull out chicken from the skillet and place on a paper-towel-lined plate to drain excess oil.

4. If needed, mix in rest of the oil to the skillet and heat over medium-high heat. When hot, stir in onions, garlic and peppers and cook until the onions and peppers start to soften.

5. When soft, return the chicken to the skillet along with the chili sauce, pineapple and pineapple juice and allow to cook for about 7 minutes, stirring occasionally. Serve with a side of rice.

Nutrition:

624 calories

11g fats

31g protein

Panda Express's Zucchini Mushroom Chicken

Preparation Time: 15 minutes

Cooking Time: 10 minutes

Servings: 4

Ingredients

- 1-pound boneless skinless chicken breasts, cut into bite-sized pieces
- 3 tablespoons cornstarch
- 1 tablespoon canola oil
- 1 tablespoon sesame oil
- ½ pound mushrooms, sliced
- 1 medium zucchini
- 1 cup broccoli florets
- ¼ cup soy sauce
- 1 tablespoon rice wine vinegar
- 2 teaspoons sugar
- 3 cloves garlic, minced
- 2 teaspoons minced ginger or ½ teaspoon ground ginger
- Sesame seeds, for garnish (optional)

Directions

1. Add the cornstarch to a shallow dish and season with salt and pepper. Add the chicken and toss to coat. In a large skillet, heat both the canola and sesame oil over medium high-heat. When hot, add the chicken and cookuntil brown on all sides.

2. Pull out chicken from the skillet and turn the heat to high. Cook the zucchini, mushrooms, and broccoli until they begin to soften, about 1 minute. Cook the garlic and ginger a bit longer. Continue to cook until the mushrooms and zucchini have softened to taste, then stir the chicken back into the skillet. When the chicken has heated up, stir in the soy sauce and the rice wine vinegar. Serve with rice.

Nutrition:

701 Calories

11g Fats

29g Protein

Panda Express's Orange Chicken

Preparation Time: 15 minutes

Cooking Time: 10 minutes

Servings: 4–6

Ingredients

- 1 egg

- 1½ teaspoons salt

- White pepper to taste

- Oil for frying

- 2 pounds boneless skinless chicken

- ½ cup cornstarch

- ¼ cup flour

- Orange sauce

- 3 tablespoons soy sauce

- ¾ cup orange juice

- ½ cup brown sugar

- Zest of 1 orange

- 1 tablespoon oil

- 2 tablespoons ginger, minced

- 2 teaspoons garlic, minced

- 1 teaspoon red chili flakes

- ½ cup green onion, chopped

- 2 tablespoons rice wine

- ½ cup water

- 2 tablespoons cornstarch

- 1 teaspoon sesame oil

Directions

1. In a shallow dish, combine the ½ cup of cornstarch and the flour. In a second shallow dish, beat together the egg, salt, pepper and 1 tablespoon of oil. In a large skillet or deep saucepan, heat oil to 375°F.

2. Soak chicken pieces in the egg mixture followed by the flour mixture. Shake off any excess flour. Situate coated chicken to the hot oil and cook for about 4 minutes or until nicely browned. Transfer the chicken from the hot oil to a paper-towel-lined plate to drain.

3. Scourge soy sauce, orange juice, brown sugar and orange zest. In another skillet or wok, heat 1 tablespoon of oil. When hot, add the ginger, garlic, red pepper flakes and green onions. Cook for 1

minute.

4. Stir in the rice wine and soy sauce mixture. Cook for about 1 more minute, then add the chicken. Make a slurry with the water and remaining cornstarch and gradually add to the skillet until the sauce thickens. Add sesame oil to taste. Serve with rice.

Ntrition:

725 Calories

12g Fats

34g Protein

Bistro Shrimp Pasta

Preparation Time: 30 Minutes

Cooking Time: 45 Minutes

Servings: 8

Ingredients:

- 2 tablespoons olive oil
- 1 cup button mushrooms, quartered
- 1 cup grape tomatoes, halved
- 1-pound thin spaghetti, cooked

For the Lemon Basil Cream Sauce

- ¼ cup butter
- 4 garlic cloves, minced
- 2 cups heavy whipping cream
- 2 cups chicken broth
- ½ cup lemon juice
- ¼ cupcornstarch
- ½ teaspoonpepper
- 1 cup chopped fresh basil

For the shrimp

- 1-pound raw shrimp, deveined and with shells removed 2 eggs, beaten
- 1 cup flour
- 1 cup panko
- 1 teaspoon garlic powder
- 1 teaspoonItalianseasoning

- 3 tablespoonsbutter

Directions:

1. In a small skillet, cook the mushrooms in 2 tablespoons of olive oil. When they are soft, stir in the tomatoes and set the skillet aside.

2. Make the cream sauce: in a large skillet, melt the butter. Add the garlic and cook until fragrant. Pour in the cream then chicken broth, and bring to a low boil. Lessen the heat and let the sauce cook until the liquid reduces by half.

3. In a small dish, whisk the corn starch into the lemon juice, mixing until it is smooth and free of lumps, making slurry. Add the slurry into the chicken broth mixture.

4. To make the shrimp, beat the eggs in one small dish and combine the panko, flour, garlic powder, and Italian seasoning in a different one. Then dip each shrimp in the egg mixture and then into the panko.

5. Using the skillet, you cooked the mushroom and tomatoes in, melt the 3

6. tablespoons of butter. When the shrimp turns nicely golden, remove it from skillet and let it drain on a plated lined with paper towel.

7. Add the fresh basil to the sauce and stir.

8. To serve, put some pasta on the plate, cover with sauce, and top with shrimp.

Nutrition:

Calories: 234

Fat: 16 g

Carbs: 81.9 g

Protein: 76. 7 g

Sodium: 656

Crispy Crab Wontons

Preparation Time: 10 Minutes

Cooking Time: 15 Minutes

Servings: 4

Ingredients:

- 4 ounces cream cheese
- 2 tablespoons sweet and sour chili sauce (plus more for serving)
- ½ teaspoons mustard
- 1 teaspoon chili garlic paste
- 1 teaspoon lemon juice
- ½ teaspoon granulated sugar
- 4 ounces crab meat
- 2 ounces sliced water chestnuts, minced
- 2 tablespoons green onions, finely chopped
- 1 ounce mozzarella cheese, grated
- 1 ounce fontina cheese, grated
- ¼ cup panko breadcrumbs
- 25 small square wonton wrappers, approximately 3-½ inches
- Oil for frying

Directions:

1. In a large bowl, mix together the cream cheese, sweet and sour sauce, mustard, garlic paste, lemon juice, and sugar.

2. Stir until well combined, then gently add in the crab, the water chestnuts, and green onions.

3. In a distinct bowl, combine the mozzarella, fontina, and panko breadcrumbs. Carefully fold them into the cream cheese combination, until well distributed.

4. Heat enough oil in a large frypan or saucepan so that the wontons won't touch the bottom when you cook them.

5. Lay out a wonton wrapper and fill it with about a teaspoon of filling.

6. Pinch the sides of the wonton up and seal with a bit of water on your fingers.

7. When the oil is about 350°F, fry the wontons until they turn a golden brown.

8. Handover them to a plate lined with paper towel to drain.

9. Serve the wontons with sweet and sour chili sauce.

Nutrition:

Calories: 724

Fat: 39 g

Carbs: 89 g

Protein: 65 g

Sodium: 1587 mg

Chicken Casserole

Preparation Time: 10 Minutes

Cooking Time: 1 Hour and 20 Minutes

Servings: 4

Ingredients:

Crust

- 1 cup yellow cornmeal
- 1/3 cup all-purpose flour
- 1½ teaspoons baking powder
- 1 tablespoon sugar
- ½ teaspoon salt
- ½ teaspoon baking soda
- 2 tablespoons vegetable oil
- ¾ cup buttermilk
- 1 egg

Filling

- 2½ cups cooked chicken breast,
- ¼ cup chopped yellow onion
- ½ cup sliced celery
- 1 teaspoon salt
- ¼ teaspoon ground pepper
- 1 can condensed cream of chicken soup
- 1¾ cups chicken broth
- 2 tablespoons butter
- ½ cup melted butter

Directions:

1. Preheat the oven to 375°F.

2. To create the crust, in a big bowl, combine all of the crust ingredients until smooth.

3. Dump this mixture into a buttered or greased 8×8-inch baking dish. Bake for about 20 minutes, then remove from oven and allow to cool. Reduce oven temperature to 350°F.

4. Crumble the cooled cornbread mixture. Add to a large mixing bowl with ½ cup of melted butter. Set aside.

5. Make the chicken filling by adding the butter to a large saucepan over medium heat. Let it melt, then add the celery and onions and cook until soft.

6. Add the chicken broth, cream of chicken soup, salt and pepper. Stir until everything is well combined. Add the cooked chicken breast pieces and stir again. Cook for 5 minutes at a low simmer. Transfer the filling mixture into 4 individual greased baking dishes or into a greased casserole dish. Top with the cornbread mixture and transfer to the oven.

7. Bake for 35–40 minutes for a large casserole dish or 25–30 minutes for individual dishes.

Nutrition:

Calories: 454

Fat: 65 g   Carbs: 98 g

Protein: 88 g   Sodium: 387 mg

Sunday Chicken

Preparation Time: 10 Minutes

Cooking Time: 10 Minutes

Servings: 4

Ingredients:

- Oil for frying
- 4 boneless, skinless chicken breasts
- 1 cup all-purpose flour
- 1 cup bread crumbs
- 2 teaspoons salt
- 2 teaspoons black pepper
- 1 cup buttermilk
- ½ cup water

Directions:

1. Add 3–4 inches of oil to a large pot or a deep fryer and preheat to 350°F.

2. Mix together the flour, breadcrumbs, salt and pepper in a shallow dish. To a separate shallow dish, add the buttermilk and water; stir.

3. Pound the chicken breasts to a consistent size. Dry them with a paper towel, at that time sprinkle with salt and pepper. Dip the seasoned breasts in the flour mixture, then the buttermilk mixture, then back into the flour. Add the breaded chicken to the oil then fry for about 8 minutes. Turn the chicken as necessary so that it cooks evenly on both sides.

4. Remove the chicken to either a wire rack or a plate lined with paper towels to drain.

5. Serve with mashed potatoes or whatever sides you love.

Nutrition:

Calories:265

Fat: 47.9 g

Carbs: 65. 5 g

Protein: 37. 4 g

Sodium: 454 mg

Creamy Chicken and Rice

Preparation Time: 10 Minutes

Cooking Time: 45 Minutes

Servings: 4

Ingredients:

- Salt and pepper to taste
- 2 cups cooked rice
- 1 diced onion
- 1 can cream of mushroom soup
- 1 packet chicken gravy
- 1½ pounds chicken breasts, cut into strips

Directions:

1. Preheat the oven to 350°F.
2. Cook the rice. When it is just about finished, toss in the diced onion so that it cooks too.
3. Prepare a baking dish by greasing or spraying with nonstick cooking spray.
4. Dump the rice into the prepared baking dish. Layer the chicken strips on top.
5. Spread the unmixed cream of mushroom soup over the chicken.
6. In a small bowl, whisk together the chicken gravy with 1 cup of water, making sure to get all the lumps out. Pour this over the casserole.
7. Cover by foil then transfer to the oven.

8. Bake for 45 minutes or pending the chicken is completely cooked.

Nutrition:

Calories: 323

Fat: 56 g

Carbs: 32.5 g

Protein: 58.7 g

Sodium: 574 mg

Campfire Chicken

Preparation Time: 10 Minutes

Cooking Time: 45 Minutes

Servings: 4

Ingredients:

- 1 tablespoon paprika
- 2 teaspoons onion powder
- 2 teaspoons salt
- 1 teaspoon garlic powder
- 1 teaspoon dried rosemary
- 1 teaspoon black pepper
- 1 teaspoon dried oregano
- 1 whole chicken, quartered
- 2 carrots, cut into thirds
- 3 red skin potatoes, halved
- 1 ear of corn, quartered
- 1 tablespoon olive oil
- 1 tablespoon butter
- 5 sprigs fresh thyme

Directions:

1. Preheat the oven to 400°F.
2. In a bowl, combine the onion powder, paprika, salt, garlic powder, rosemary, pepper and oregano.
3. Add the chicken quarters and 1 tablespoon of the spice mix to a large plastic freezer bag.

4. Seal and chill for at minimum 1 hour. Add the corn, carrots and potatoes to a large bowl.

5. Drizzle with the olive oil and remaining spice mix. Stir or toss to coat. Preheat a large skillet over high heat.

6. Add some oil, and when it is hot, add the chicken pieces and cook until golden brown.

7. Lay out 4 pieces of aluminum foil then add some carrots, potatoes, corn and a chicken quarter to each.

8. Top with some butter and thyme.

9. Fold the foil in and make pouches by sealing the edges tightly.

10. Bake for 45 minutes.

Nutrition:

Calories: 234

Fat: 54. 4 g

Carbs: 67. 9 g

Protein: 76. 5

Sodium: 652 mg

Chicken and Dumplings

Preparation Time: 30 Minutes

Cooking Time: 20 Minutes

Servings: 4

Ingredients:

- 2 cups flour
- ½ teaspoon baking powder 1 pinch salt
- 2 tablespoons butter 1 scant cup buttermilk
- 2 quarts chicken broth
- 3 cups cooked chicken

Directions:

1. Make the dumplings by compounding the flour, baking powder and salt in a large bowl. By means of a pastry cutter or two knives, cut the butter into the flour mixture. Stir in the milk a tiny at a time until it forms a dough ball.

2. Cover your countertop with enough flour that the dough will not stick when you roll it out. Roll out the dough relatively thin, then cut into squares to form dumplings.

3. Flour a plate and transfer the dough from the counter to the plate.

4. Bring the chicken broth to a boil in a large saucepan, then drop the dumplings in one by one, stirring continually. The excess flour will thicken the broth.

5. Cook for about 20 minutes or pending the dumplings are no longer doughy.

6.   Add the chicken, stir to combine, and serve.

Nutrition:

Calories: 323

Fat: 78g

Carbs: 87 g

Protein: 69 g

 Sodium: 769 mg

Chicken Pot Pie

Preparation Time: 30 Minutes

Cooking Time: 30 Minutes

Servings: 8

Ingredients:

- ½ cup butter
- 1 medium onion, diced
- 1 (14.5-ounce) can chicken broth
- 1 cup half and half milk
- ½ cup all-purpose flour
- 1 carrot, diced
- 1 celery stalk, diced
- 3 medium potatoes, peeled and diced
- 3 cups cooked chicken, diced
- ½ cup frozen peas
- 1 teaspoon chicken seasoning
- ½ teaspoon salt
- ½ teaspoon ground pepper
- 1 single refrigerated pie crust
- 1 egg
- Water

Directions:

1. Preheat the oven to 375°F.
2. In a large frypan, heat the butter over medium heat, add the leeks and sauté for 3 minutes.

3. Sprinkle flour over the mixture, and remain to stir constantly for 3 minutes.
4. Whisking constantly, blend in the chicken broth and milk. Bring the mixture to a boil. Reduce heat to medium-low.
5. Add the carrots, celery, potatoes, salt, pepper, and stir to combine. Cook for 10-15 minutes or pending veggies are cooked through but still crisp. Add chicken and peas. Stir to combine.
6. Transfer chicken filling to a deep 9-inch pie dish.
7. Fit the pie crust sheet on top and press the edges around the dish to seal the crust. Trim the excess if needed.
8. In a distinct bowl, whisk an egg with 1 tablespoon of water, and brush the mixture over the top of the pie. With a knife, cut a few slits to let steam escape.
9. Bake the pie in the oven on the middle oven rack 20 to 30 minutes until the crust becomes golden brown.
10. Let the pie rest for about 15 minutes before serving.

Nutrition:

Calories: 125

Fat: 43 g

Carbs: 76 g

Protein: 65 g

Sodium: 545 mg

Chang's Mongolian Beef

Preparation Time: 10 Minutes

Cooking Time: 20 Minutes

Servings: 2

Ingredients:

- 1 pound flank steak
- ¼ cup cornstarch
- 2 teaspoons
- ½ teaspoon ginger, finely chopped
- 1 tablespoon ginger, diced
- ½ soy sauce
- ½ cup water
- ½ cup brown sugar
- 1 cup vegetable oil, divided
- 6 green onions, cut diagonally into 2-inch pieces

Directions:

1. Cut steak against the grain into small pieces, about ¼ inch. Transfer steak into a bowl with cornstarch and flip until fully coated on all sides. Set aside.

2. In a frypan, heat 1 tablespoon of the oil on medium heat. Stir in ginger and garlic. Cook for about 1 minute or pending aromatic. Mix in soy sauce, water, and brown sugar. Keep stirring until sugar is melted. Bring to a boil on medium heat. Simmer for around 2 minutes or until sauce is thick.

3. Heat remaining vegetable oil in a separate saucepan on medium heat until oil reaches 350 F. Deep-fry steak in batches for 2 minutes or until brown.
4. Handover onto a plate lined with paper towels.
5. Discard the oil, then add sauce and stir in meat with sauce in saucepan for about 2 minutes on medium heat. Mix in green onions and cook for an
6. additional 1-2 minute. Place meat and onions on a plate.
7. Serve hot.

Nutrition:

Calories: 847

Fat: 24 g

Carbs: 103 g

Protein: 57 g

Sodium: 4176 mg

Panda Express' Beijing Beef

Preparation Time: 30 Minutes

Cooking Time: 15 Minutes

Servings: 4

Ingredients:

- 1 egg
- ¼ teaspoon salt
- 6 tablespoons water
- 9 tablespoons cornstarch
- 1 pound flank steak
- 4 tablespoons sugar
- 3 tablespoons ketchup
- 2 tablespoons vinegar
- ¼ teaspoon chili pepper, crushed
- 1 cup vegetable oil
- 1 teaspoon garlic, finely chopped
- 1 red bell pepper, chopped
- 1 green bell pepper, chopped
- 1 white onion, chopped

Directions:

1. To make the marinade, add egg, salt, 2 tablespoons water, and 1 tablespoon cornstarch in a bowl. Mix well.
2. Slice steak counter to the grain into small strips.
3. Transfer into a Ziploc bag and pour marinade inside. Seal tightly.

4. Shake bag gently to make sure the meat is well-coated. Set aside for at least 15 minutes.

5. To make the sauce, combine sugar, ketchup, vinegar, chili pepper, remaining 4 tablespoons water, and 2 teaspoons cornstarch in a bowl. Mix well.

6. Cover and keep refrigerated. Heat oil in a saucepan. Ready a bowl with 6 tablespoons cornstarch.

7. Place beef in bowl and toss until fully coated.

8. Shake off excess cornstarch and cook beef in hot oil until golden brown. Handover onto a plate lined with paper towels.

9. Remove excess oil from saucepan.

10. Toss in garlic, bell peppers, and onions and cook for about 2 minutes, stirring continuously.

11. Transfer vegetables onto a plate. In the same saucepan, add sauce and bring to a boil. Reduce heat to low and let simmer for 10 minutes.

12. Serve beef and vegetables with sauce poured on top.

Nutrition:

Calories: 352

Fat: 11 g

Carbs: 36 g

Protein: 27 g

Sodium: 355 mg

Chili from Steak n' Shak

Preparation Time: 20 Minutes

Cooking Time: 6 Minutes

Servings: 6

Ingredients:

- 1 tablespoon olive oil
- 2 pounds ground beef
- ½ teaspoon salt
- 2 tablespoons onion powder
- 1 tablespoon chili powder
- 2 teaspoons ground cumin
- ½ teaspoon ground black pepper
- 2 teaspoons cocoa powder
- 6 ounces canned tomato paste
- 13½ ounces canned tomato sauce
- 1 cup Pepsi
- 27 ounces canned kidney beans,
- Shredded cheese, sliced green onions for toppings, if desired

Directions:

1. Heat oil in a pan. Add beef and cook until brown, drain, then remove from heat.

2. In a bowl, add cooked meat, salt, onion powder, chili powder, cumin, pepper, cocoa powder, tomato paste, tomato sauce, and Pepsi. Mix until combined.

3. Pour combination into a blender and puree until well blended.
4. Add mixture into slow cooker. Pour in beans. Cover and set slow cooker to low set and cook for 6 hours.
5. Serve with shredded cheese and green onions, if desired, on top.

Nutrition:

Calories: 653

Fat: 41 g

Saturated fat: 17 g

Carbs: 38 g

Sugar: 12 g

Fibers: 11 g

Protein: 35 g

Sodium: 1308 mg

Cracker Barrel's Meatloaf

Preparation Time: 10 Minutes

Cooking Time: 1 Hour and 10 Minutes

Servings: 4

Ingredients:

- 1 pound ground beef
- 1 onion, chopped
- 1 green pepper, chopped
- 1 can chopped tomatoes
- 1 egg
- ½ cup frozen biscuits, shredded
- 1 teaspoon salt
- ¼ cup ketchup (optional)
- Non-stick cooking spray

Directions:

1. Preheat oven to 350°F.
2. In a bowl, add beef, onion, green pepper, tomatoes, egg, biscuits, and salt.
3. Mix well.
4. Using a non-stick cooking spray, coat bread pan. Then, pour meatloaf mixture into pan. Make sure the mixture is even and flat in the pan.
5. Place in oven then bake for approximately 1 hour and 5 minutes or until cooked through. Take away from oven then allow to cool for about 10 minutes.

6. Drain excess juice, then invert cooked meatloaf onto a serving plate. Drizzle ketchup on top, if desired. Serve.

Nutrition:

Calories: 485

Fat: 32 g

Saturated fat: 13 g

Carbs: 27 g

Sugar: 3 g

Fibers: 1 g

Protein: 23 g

Sodium: 1273 mg

Sizzling Steak, Cheese, and Mushrooms Skillet from Applebee's

Preparation Time: 15 Minutes

Cooking Time: 1 Hour and 35 Minutes

Servings: 4

Ingredients:

- 1 head garlic, cut crosswise
- 2 tablespoons olive oil, divided
- Salt and pepper, to taste
- 2 pounds Yukon Gold potatoes,
- Water, for boiling
- 2 tablespoons butter
- 1 large yellow onion
- 8 ounces cremini mushrooms
- Salt and pepper to taste
- ½ cup milk
- ¼ cup cream
- 3 tablespoons butter
- 2½ pounds 1-inch-thick sirloin steak, cut into 4 large pieces
- 8 slices mozzarella cheese

Directions:

1. Preheat oven to 300°F.

2. Position garlic on foil. Pour 1 tablespoon olive oil to the inner sides where the garlic was cut, then wrap foil around garlic.

3. Put it in oven then bake for 30 minutes. Remove from oven, and squeeze out garlic from head. Transfer to a bowl or mortar. Add salt and pepper, then mash together. Set aside.

4. In a pot, add potatoes. Pour enough water on top to cover potatoes. Bring to a boil. Once boiling, reduce heat to medium. Simmer for about 20 to 25

5. minutes or until potatoes become tender.

6. Melt butter on a non-stick pan over medium-low heat. Add onions and sauté for about 15 minutes until a bit tender. Toss in mushrooms and sauté, adjusting heat to medium. Season with salt and pepper. Cook for 10 minutes more. Set aside and keep warm.

7. Drain potatoes, then mash using an electric mixer on low speed. While mashing, gradually pour in milk, cream, butter, and mashed garlic with olive oil. Keep blending until everything is cream-like and smooth. Remove from mixer and place a cover on top of bowl. Set aside and keep warm.

8. Evenly coat steak pieces with remaining 1 tablespoon olive oil on all sides.

9. Heat grill, then place meat on grill. Cook for 4 minutes. Flip and add mozzarella slices on top. Cook for additional 4 minutes for medium rare. Add additional minutes for increased doneness.
10. Transfer steaks to serving plates then top with onion/mushroom mixture.
11. Place mashed potatoes on the side. Serve.

Nutrition:

Calories: 1159

Fat: 60 g

Saturated fat: 29 g

Carbs: 47 g

Sugar: 4 g

Fibers: 6 g

Protein: 107 g

Sodium: 1495 mg

Panda Express' Beef and Broccoli

Preparation Time: 30 Minutes

Cooking Time: 15 Minutes

Servings: 4

Ingredients:

- 2 tablespoons cornstarch, divided
- 3 tablespoons Chinese rice wine, divided
- 1 pound flank steak, cut thinly against the grain
- 1 pound broccoli florets,
- 2 tablespoons oyster sauce
- 2 tablespoons water
- 1 tablespoon brown sugar
- 1 tablespoon soy sauce
- 1 tablespoon cornstarch
- 2 tablespoons canola oil
- ¼ teaspoon sesame oil
- 1 teaspoon ginger, finely chopped
- 2 cloves garlic, finely chopped
- 2 teaspoons sesame seeds

Directions:

1. In a big Ziploc bag, add 1 tablespoon cornstarch and 2 tablespoons Chinese rice wine. Place beef inside and seal tightly. Massage bag to fully coat beef.
2. Set aside to marinate for at minimum 20 minutes.

3. Rinse broccoli and place in a nonreactive bowl. Put a wet paper towel, then microwave for 2 minutes. Set aside.

4. Stir oyster sauce, water, 1 tablespoon Chinese rice wine, brown sugar, soy sauce, and remaining cornstarch in a bowl until well mixed. Set aside.

5. Heat wok over high heat. You want the wok to be very hot. Then, heat canola and sesame oil in wok and wait to become hot. Working in batches, add steak and cook over high heat for 1 minute. Flip, then cook other side for extra 1 minute. Transfer to a plate.

6. To the same wok, add garlic and ginger. Sauté for about 10 to 15 seconds then return beef to wok. Toss in heated broccoli. Slightly stir prepared sauce to make sure cornstarch is not settled on the bottom, then add to wok. Toss everything in sauce to combine. Continue cooking until sauce becomes thick.

7. Garnish with sesame seeds. Serve.

Nutrition:

Calories: 324

Fat: 17 g

Saturated fat: 4g

Carbs: 13 g

Sugar: 6g

Fibers: 3 g

Protein: 28 g

Sodium: 464 mg

Jack Daniel's Ribs from TGI Fridays

Preparation Time: 15 Minutes

Cooking Time: 5 Minutes

Servings: 4

Ingredients:

- 1 head garlic
- 1 tablespoon olive oil 1½ teaspoons paprika
- ½ teaspoon salt ¼ teaspoon dried thyme
- ½ teaspoon ground black pepper
- ½ teaspoon garlic powder
- ½ teaspoon onion powder
- ¼ teaspoon celery salt
- ¼ teaspoon ground cayenne pepper
- 2 racks baby back ribs
- ½ cup water
- 1 cup pineapple juice
- ¼ cup teriyaki sauce
- 1 tablespoon soy sauce
- 1 1/3 cups dark brown sugar
- 3 tablespoons lemon juice
- ¼ cup white onion, finely chopped
- 2 tablespoons Jack Daniel's whiskey
- 1 heaping tablespoon pineapple, crushed
- ¼ teaspoon cayenne pepper

Directions:

1. Preheat oven to 300°F.
2. Take garlic and chop off around ½ inches from the head. Take out paper-like outer layers then put it in a small oven-safe container or ramekin. Pour olive oil
3. on top and wrap in aluminum foil.
4. Put it in oven and bake for 1 hour. When prepared, remove from oven and allow to cool. Crush out about garlic from roasted garlic head. Add roasted garlic in an airtight vessel and place in refrigerator
5. Whereas the garlic is baking, prepare the spice rub by joining paprika, salt, thyme, onion powder, pepper, garlic powder, celery salt, and ground cayenne pepper in a bowl. Mix well. Evenly coat ribs with spice rub. Arrange ribs onto a baking sheet. Bake in oven for approximately 2½ hours.
6. Prepare the barbecue sauce by mixing water, teriyaki sauce, pineapple juice, soy sauce, and dark brown sugar in a pot. Let it boil while stirring. When boiling, lower heat until combination is just seething.
7. Add to pan 2 teaspoons of the cooked garlic, crushed pineapple, onion, whiskey, lemon juice, and cayenne pepper. Stir to combine well. Simmer for about 30 to 40 minutes until liquid is reduced by half.

8. If wanted, you can finish the ribs on the barbecue to have grilling marks and crisper ribs. Preheat grill to medium-high heat.

9. Place ribs onto grill and cook for about 2 to 4 minutes. Turn ribs over and grill for another 2 to 4 minutes.

10. Transfer onto a serving plate. Spoon sauce over ribs. Serve.

Nutrition:

Calories: 779

Fat: 38 g

 Saturated fat: 13 g

Carbs: 80 g

Sugar: 77 g

Fibers: 1 g

Protein: 29 g

Sodium: 865 mg

Smokehouse Pork Belly Sandwich from Arby's

Preparation Time: 15 Minutes

Cooking Time: 2 Hours and 30 Minutes

Servings: 6

Ingredients:

- 2 pounds center cut pork belly
- Salt and pepper, to taste
- 1-2 tablespoons barbecue spice rub
- 6-star cross buns
- Cooking spray
- ½ pound smoked cheddar cheese
- ½ cup mayonnaise
- ½ cup any smoky barbecue sauce
- 6 ounces onion strings

Directions:

1. Sprinkle salt and pepper onto pork belly then coat with barbecue rub.

2. Set smoker to 300°F with hickory wood on coals. Put pork belly in smoker with fat side facing down.

3. Smoke for about 2½ hours until well browned and a bit charred. Pork is ready once its internal temperature is about 185 to 195°F.

4. Spray cooking spray onto the inner sides of buns then toast until golden brown.

5. Assemble sandwich by layering mayo, cooked pork belly, barbecue sauce, cheese, and onion strings on the bottom bun. Top with second bun. Repeat for remaining sandwiches.
6. Serve.

Nutrition:

Calories: 1351

Fat: 117 g

Saturated fat: 41 g

Carbs: 45 g

Sugar: 13 g

Fibers: 2 g

Protein: 29 g

Sodium: 1023 mg

Red Beans and Rice from Popeye's

Preparation Time: 20 Minutes

Cooking Time: 40 Minutes

Servings: 10

Ingredients:

- 3 14-ounce cans red beans
- ¾ pounds smoked ham hock
- 1¼ cups water
- ½ teaspoon onion powder
- ½ teaspoon garlic salt
- ¼ teaspoon red pepper flakes
- ½ teaspoon salt
- 3 tablespoons lard
- Steamed long-grain rice

Directions:

1. Add 2 canned red beans, ham hock, and water to pot. Cook on medium heat and let simmer for about 1 hour.

2. Remove from heat and wait until meat is cool enough to handle. Then, remove meat from bone.

3. In a food processor, add meat, cooked red beans and water mixture, onion powder, garlic salt, red pepper, salt, and lard. Pulse for 4 seconds. You want the beans to be cut and the liquid thickened. Drain remaining 1 can red beans and add to food processor. Pulse for only 1 or 2 seconds.

4. Remove fixings from food processor then transfer to the pot from earlier.

5. Cook on low heat, stirring frequently until mixture is heated through.

6. Serve over steamed rice.

Nutrition:

Calories: 445

Fat: 12 g

Saturated fat: 4g

Carbs: 67 g

Sugar: 1 g

Fibers: 9 g

Protein: 17 g

Sodium: 670 mg

Café Rio's Sweet Pork Barbacoa Salad

Preparation Time: 10 Minutes

Cooking Time: 8 Minutes

Servings: 8

Ingredients:

- 3 pounds pork loin
- Garlic salt, to taste
- 1 can root beer
- ¼ cup water
- ¾ cup brown sugar
- 1 10-ounce can red enchilada sauce
- 1 4-ounce can green chilies
- ½ teaspoon chili powder
- 8 large burrito size tortillas
- 1½ serving Cilantro Lime Rice
- 1 can black beans, drained and heated
- 2 heads Romaine lettuce, shredded
- 1½ cups tortilla strips
- 1 cup Queso Fresco cheese
- 2 limes, cut in wedges
- ¼ cup cilantro

Dressing:

- ½ packet Hidden Valley Ranch Dressing
- ½ cup milk
- ½ cup cilantro leaves

- ¼ cup salsa Verde
- ½ jalapeno pepper, deseeded
- 1 plump clove garlic
- 2 tablespoons fresh lime juice

Directions:

1. Sprinkle garlic salt on pork. Put in slow cooker with the fat side facing down.

2. Add ¼ cup root beer and water. Cover then cook on low setting for 6 hours.

3. To prepare sauce add the rest of the root beer, brown sugar, enchilada sauce, green chilies, and chili powder in a blender. Blend until smooth.

4. Remove meat from slow cooker then transfer onto cutting board. Shred, discarding juices and fat. Return shredded pork to slow cooker with sauce.

5. Cook on low setting for another 2 hours. When there is only about 15 to 20

6. minutes left to cook, remove lid to thicken sauce.

7. To prepare dressing mix all dressing ingredients in a blender. Puree until smooth. Then, transfer to refrigerator and allow to chill for at least 1 hour.

8. To assemble salad, layer tortilla, rice, beans, pork, lettuce, tortilla strips, cheese, and dressing in a bowl. Serve with a lime wedge and cilantro leaves.

Nutrition:

Calories: 756

Fat: 28 g

Saturated fat: 7 g

Carbs: 91 g

Sugar: 31 g

Fibers: 7 g

Protein: 38 g

Sodium: 1389 mg

Edo Japan's Sukiyaki Beef

Preparation Time: 15 Minutes

Cooking Time: 5 to 6 Minutes

Servings: 4

Ingredients:

- 10 ounces sirloin steak, thinly sliced
- ½ carrot, thinly sliced
- ½ onion, sliced
- 1 green pepper, sliced
- ½ yellow bell pepper, sliced
- ½ cup sukiyaki sauce, divided
- 1 tablespoon oil
- 1 teaspoon chopped garlic
- 2 tablespoons ginger, finely chopped
- 2 teaspoons soy sauce
- 1 teaspoon sugar
- 1 tablespoon oyster sauce

Directions:

1. Pour half of the sukiyaki sauce into a medium bowl and add the sliced beef.
2. Let the beef marinate for 20 minutes.
3. Heat the oil in a large skillet. Add the garlic and cook for about 30 seconds.
4. Add the beef, with the sauce. Cook over medium-high heat until the beef is cooked through.

5. Add the ginger, carrots, peppers and onions and cook until the veggies have begun to soften.

6. Add the rest of the sukiyaki sauce along with the oyster sauce, soy sauce and sugar. Cook and stir for around 2 more minutes.

7. Serve over rice.

Nutrition:

Calories: 152

Fat:24 g

Carbs: 20 g

Protein: 5.6 g

Sodium: 627 mg

Broccoli Cheddar Chicken

Preparation Time: 10 Minutes

Cooking Time: 45 Minutes

Servings: 4

Ingredients:

- 4 skinless chicken breasts
- 1 cup milk
- 1 cup Ritz-style crackers, crushed
- 1 can condensed cheddar cheese soup ½ pound frozen broccoli
- 6 ounces cheddar cheese, shredded
- ½ teaspoon salt
- ½ teaspoon pepper

Directions:

1. Preheat the oven to 350°F.
2. Whisk the milk and cheddar cheese soup together in a mixing bowl.
3. Prepare a baking dish by greasing the sides, then lay the chicken in the bottom and season with the salt and pepper.
4. Pour the soup combination over the chicken, then top with the crackers, broccoli and shredded cheese.
5. Bake for around 45 minutes or until bubbly.

Nutrition:

Calories: 343

Fat: 43 g

Carbs: 54 g

 Protein: 16 g

Sodium: 565 mg

Chapter 2
Meat Recipes

The Southern Charm Burger

Preparation Time: 15 minutes

Cooking Time: 30 minutes

Servings: 4

Ingredients

- 2 pounds ground bison or beef

- 1 tablespoon Texas Pete or Tabasco

- 4 garlic cloves, minced

- 1 small onion, minced

- BBQ Sauce with Honey and Molasses for basting

- 8 ounces container pimento cheese spread

- 1 pc. green tomato

- ¼ cup corn meal, sprinkled with salt and pepper

- 1 large egg, beaten

- Pickled okra for condiments

- 8 Hearty Buns

- Nonstick cooking spray

Directions

1. Preheat oven at 350 degrees. Mix the egg with a small amount of water in a shallow bowl & then, season with pepper and salt to taste. Place the corn meal out onto a medium-sized plate.

2. Before cooking, soak the tomato slices into the egg and then press into the corn meal; ensure that the outside is nicely coated. Place the slices onto the baking sheet lightly coated with the cooking spray. Spray tops of tomatoes with the cooking spray. Bake for 13 minutes, turning once during the baking process.

3. Combine the ground beef together with onions, tabasco, and garlic in a large-sized mixing bowl. Season the meat well; combine thoroughly. Make 8 even-sized patties from the mixture. Baste with the BBQ Sauce & grilluntil you get your desired doneness.

4. Just about a minute before you remove the patties from grill, place a portion of pimento cheese spread on top of burgers using a cookie scoop. For even melting; press the cheese down using a large spatula. Place one "fried" green tomato over each bun, top with burger and garnish with your favorite condiments.

Nutrition:

893 Calories

58g Total Fats

40g Protein

Ihop's Banzai Burger

Preparation Time: 15 minutes

Cooking Time: 50 minutes

Servings: 2

Ingredients

- 1 large beefsteak tomato, cut into slices

- 2 beef patties

- 1 batch Homemade Teriyaki Sauce

- Fresh lettuce, shredded

- 4 pineapple rings

- Mayonnaise

- 2 slices of cheddar cheese

- Pepper & salt to taste

Directions

1. Brush the beef patties on both sides with teriyaki sauce. Grill until you get your desired doneness; basting occasionally with the teriyaki sauce. Situate cheese on top near the end to melt. Brush the pineapple rings on both sides with the teriyaki sauce & grill for a minute on each side.

2. Lightly toast the hamburger buns. Place the patties over

the bottom bun, place two slices of tomatoes & then two pineapple rings on top. Brush the pineapple rings with more of teriyaki sauce. Top with the shredded lettuce. Lay out generous amount of mayonnaise on the top bun & place it on the hamburger. Serve immediately and enjoy.

Nutrition:

911 Calories

60.3g Total Fats

41.9g Protein

Mcdonald's Burnin' Love Burger

Preparation Time: 10 minutesCooking Time: 20 minutes Servings: 1

Ingredients

- 1 jalapeno Kaiser cornmeal roll

- Chipotle mayonnaise

- 1/3-pound ground beef 80% lean or above, made into a patty

- Iceberg lettuce shredded

- Cayenne seasoning

- 2 slices pepper-jack cheese

- Salsa

- 1 tomato vine ripened, sliced

- Fresh Jalapeno rings or battered & fried

- Pepper & salt to taste

Directions

1. For Chipotle Mayonnaise:

2. Combine the mayonnaise with pureed chipotle peppers, pepper and salt to taste. To enhance the flavor;

refrigerate for an hour.

3. For the Salsa:

4. Enhance your favorite store-bought salsa with fresh finely chopped tomatoes, cilantro, red onion, jalapenos and Serrano peppers.

For the Burger:

1. Season the patty with cayenne, pepper and salt to taste. Oil the grill grates & preheat it.

2. Grill the patty for a couple of seconds; flip and grill the other side too until cooked through. Remove the burger from grill & top with the pepper-jack cheese. Grill for two more minutes until the cheese is completely melted. Toast the bun on the grill until turn goldenbrown.

3. Lay out chipotle mayonnaise on both sides of your toasted bun. Place the burger on the bun & top with sliced tomato, jalapenos, salsa & shredded lettuce. Cover with the bun top; serve immediately & enjoy.

Nutrition

897 Calories

58.9g Total Fats

40.9g Protein

Starbuck Red Robin Burger

Preparation Time: 10 minutes

Cooking Time: 30 minutes

Servings: 4

Ingredients

- 4 toasted buns or 4 toast

- 1 ½ pounds lean hamburger

- 4 large eggs, fried over-medium

- Fresh coarse ground black pepper & seasoning salt to taste

- 8 slices American cheese

- ketchup

- 4 slices bacon, cooked and cut in half

- Fresh lettuce

- 4 slices tomatoes

- Mayonnaise

Directions

1. Cook the bacon until done; set aside to cool. Once done; break into half. Make 4 even-sized patties from of the beef and then season with pepper and sal to taste; pan-

fry or grill in a small amount of bacon fat until done.

2. Place each patty with a slice of cheese, cover lightly & set aside. Fry the eggs to your liking sunny-side up, over medium heat. Toast the buns. When done; set aside. Assemble your burger in the following order:

3. Bottom bun next slice of cheese, fried egg, a small amount of ketchup, 2 pieces of bacon, tomato, fresh lettuce & top the bun, spread with mayo.

4. Serve with French fries or hash browns and enjoy.

Nutrition:

904 Calories

62.4g Total Fats

40.1g Protein

Sautéed Mushroom Burger

Preparation Time: 10 minutes

Cooking Time: 20 minutes

 Servings: 4

Ingredients

- 1 lb. ground hamburger

- Garlic salt to taste

- Onion powder to taste

- Seasoned salt to taste

- 2 c. sliced mushrooms

- 1 tbsp. butter

- ½ onion caramelized

- 4 slices Swiss cheese

- Lettuce

Directions

1. Preheat your grill over medium-high heat. Evenlydivide the hamburger into eight balls. Flatten & season both sides with pepper & salt to taste. Grill until you getyour desired doneness. Once done; remove them from the heat. Caramelize the onions & sauté the mushrooms

with butter until tender; set aside. Once burger is done, top with onions, lettuce, mushrooms, & cheese.

Nutrition:

891 Calories

58.9 Total Fats

37.9g Protein

Whisky River Burger

Preparation Time: 20 minutes

Cooking Time: 20 minutes

Servings: 6

Ingredients

- 2 pounds 80/20 ground beef

- 6 slices of cheddar cheese

- Oil, for brushing the burgers

- 12 tablespoon mayonnaise

- Onion rings, thin & crispy

- 6 seeded hamburger buns

- Bourbon whiskey BBQ sauce

- 2 cups fresh lettuce, chopped

- 12 slices tomato

Directions

2. Preheat the charcoal grill over high heat until it glows bright orange & ashes over.
3. In the meantime, make 6 even-sized patties from the ground beef. Lightly brush the burgers with oil.

Grill the burgers for 7 minutes. Flip & continue cooking until you get your desired level of doneness. Drizzle the Bourbon Whiskey BBQ Sauce over the burgers & place one slice of cheese on each burger. Cook a minute more. Remove from the heat; set aside and assemble the burgers.

4. Layer the cut side of both parts of the bun with approximately 1 tablespoon of mayonnaise on each half. Place the Onion Rings over the cut side of the bottom bun portion. Add the burger with cheese and sauce. Top with lettuce and tomatoes. Serve immediately & enjoy.

Nutrition:

893 Calories

57.8g Total Fats

40.4g Protein

Cracker barrel's Tuscan Butter Burger

Preparation Time: 15 minutes

Cooking Time: 30 minutes

Servings: 4

Ingredients

For the Chicken Burgers

- 1 cup panko

- 1 ½ pounds ground chicken

- 4 green onions, minced

- 2 tablespoon extra-virgin olive oil

- 1 teaspoon Himalayan pink salt, black pepper, garlic blend

For the Tuscan Butter Sauce

- ¼ cup Parmesan, finely grated

- 2 tablespoon butter

- ½ cup heavy cream

- 1 tablespoon tomato paste

- ¼ teaspoon Himalayan pink salt, black pepper, garlic

blend

For Assembly

- 4 seeded hamburger buns, split & lightly toasted

- 1 cup large basil leaves, fresh

- 1 jar oil-packed sun-dried tomatoes (7-ounces), drained

Directions

1. For Chicken Burgers: Combine the chicken together with panko, green onions & 1 teaspoon Himalayan pink salt, garlic blend, black pepper in a medium bowl.

2. Cook oil over medium-high heat in a large skillet. Form

   4 even-sized patties from the chicken mixture using slightly dampened hands, placing the patties carefully into the hot skillet. Cook for 8 to 10 minutes, until turn golden, flipping once during the cooking time. Remove the patties to a large plate; drain any excess oil.

3. For Tuscan butter Sauce: Place the skillet over medium-low heat & add butter & tomato paste. Cook for a minute, whisking frequently. Whisk in the Parmesan, heavy cream & 1/4 teaspoon

Himalayan pink salt, black pepper, garlic blend. Bring the mixture to a simmer. Once done; decrease the heat to low & let simmer until parmesan is melted & the sauce is reduced slightly, for a couple of more minutes. Remove from the heat.

4. Place the burger patties on the bottom buns. Spoon the Tuscan butter sauce on top of patties and then top with sun-dried tomatoes and basil. Close the sandwich with top bun.

Nutrition:

897 Calories

60g Total Fats

40g Protein

Red lobster Four Cheese Melt

Preparation Time: 10 minutes

Cooking Time: 30 minutes

Servings: 4

Ingredients

- 1 cup Asiago, shredded

- 2 tbsp. extra-virgin olive oil

- 1 garlic clove

- 8 slices of crusty Italian semolina bread

- 1 cup mozzarella

- ½ cup Romano or Parmesan, grated

- 1 cup provolone, shredded

- 3 tablespoons butter

Directions

1. Over medium low heat in a small skillet; heat the oil with butter. Once the butter is completely melted; add the garlic & gently cook for 2 to 3 minutes. Remove the garlic butter mixture from heat. Now, over medium high heat in a large nonstick skillet. Brush 1 side of 4 slices of bread with garlic oil using a pastry brush & place the buttered side down into the hot skillet. Top each slice with

equal amounts of the 4 cheeses; evenly distributing them over the 4 slices. Top each sandwich with a slice more of bread brushed with garlic butter, buttered side up. Flip the grill cheese sandwiches a couple of times until cheeses are melted & gooey and bread is toasty & golden. Cut grilled 4 cheese sandwiches from corner to corner; serve and enjoy.

Nutrition:

904 Calories

61g Total Fats

40.9g Protein

Pub Mac N Cheese Entree

Preparation Time: 20 minutes

Cooking Time: 30 minutes

Servings: 4

Ingredients

- 8 ounces dry pasta

- 2 tablespoon flour

- 4 tablespoon butter

- 6 ounces beer (we used an IPA)

- 1 tablespoon coarse-ground mustard

- ¼ cup milk

- 6 ounces sharp cheddar cheese, shredded

- 1 cup soft pretzel, diced into ¼" pieces

- 3 ounces Monterey jack cheese, shredded

Directions

1. Boil the pasta per the directions mentioned on the package Drain & set aside Now, over moderate heat in a large saucepan; heat 2 tablespoon of butter & mix in 2 tablespoons of flour; cook for a minute or two.

2. Add beer; give the ingredients a good stir until

combined well. Add milk & cook until thickened slightly, for 5 minutes, stirring frequently. Add mustard& cheese; decreases the heat to low.

3. Now, over moderate heat in a separate pan; heat 2 tablespoon of butter & add in the chopped pretzels, stir to coat nicely with the butter. Combine pasta with cheese sauce; transfer to an oven safe container & bake for 15 minutes at 350 F.

4. Remove from the oven & sprinkle with pretzel pieces; place into the oven again & bake for 15 minutes more. Serve hot & enjoy.

Nutrition:

894 Calories

55g Total Fats

37g Protein

The Boss Burger

Preparation Time: 15 minutes

Cooking Time: 25 minutes

Servings: 3

Ingredients

- 1-pound ground beef

- 3 cheese slices

- Worcestershire sauce

- 3 fried eggs

- canned green chilis or Verde green sauce (any of yourfavorite)

- 6 bacon slices, cooked until crisp

- Pico de Gallo

- 3 burger buns

- Pepper & salt to taste

Directions

1. Heat your grill over high heat. Season the ground beef with dashes of Worcestershire sauce, pepper & salt. Make 3 patties from the mixture & cook until you get your desired level of doneness. During the last minuteof your cooking time; top each burger with a cheese

slice. Place on a bun topped with an egg, bacon, a big scoop of Pico de Gallo & a scoop of Verde sauce.

2. Serve immediately & enjoy.

Nutrition:

889 Calories

60g Total Fats

40g Protein

Alex's Santa Fe Burger

Preparation Time: 15 minutes

Cooking Time: 15 minutes

Servings: 4

Ingredients

For Burgers:

- 12 yellow or blue corn tortilla chips

- 1 poblano chili, large

- 4 hamburger buns, split; toasted

- 1 ½ pounds 80% lean ground chuck or 90% lean ground turkey

- 2 ½ tablespoons canola oil For Queso Sauce:

- 1 tablespoon all-purpose flour

- 2 cups Monterey Jack cheese, Coarsely grated (approximately 8 ounces)

- 1 tablespoon unsalted butter

- 1 ½ cups whole milk

Directions

Preheat oven to 375 F. Put the chili on a rimmed baking sheet; rub with a tablespoon of the oil & then season with pepper and salt to taste. Roast in the preheated oven for 12 to 15 minutes, until the skin of the chili is blackened. Remove & place the chili in a large bowl; cover using a plastic wrap & let steam for 12 to 15 more minutes. Peel, stem & seed the chili then chop it coarsely.

1. For Queso Sauce: Heat the butter over medium heat in a small saucepan until completely melted. Mix in the flour then cook for a minute. Add the milk; stir well and increase the heat to high; cook for 3 to 5 minutes, until thickened slightly, whisking constantly. Remove from the heat & whisk in the cheese until melted then season with pepper and salt. Try to keep it warm.

2. Evenly divide the meat into 4 portions. Loosely form each portion into a ¾" thick burger & make a deep depression in the middle with your thumb. Sprinkle both sides of each burger with pepper and salt. Cook the burgers in the leftover oil

3. Situate burgers on the bun bottoms & top each with chips, a few tablespoons of queso sauce & some of the poblano. Cover with the bun tops; serve immediately & enjoy.

4. For Toasted Burger Buns:

   To toast a bun on a grill, griddle or grill pan; split the bun open and situate it on the grill, cut side down; grill for a couple of seconds, until turn golden brown lightly.

Nutrition:

891 Calories

62 Total Fats

41g Protein

Chili's Avocado Beef Burger

Preparation Time: 20 minutes
Cooking Time: 20 minutes
Servings: 4

Ingredients

- 1-pound ground beef

- 8 sliced crispy cooked bacon

- 1 teaspoon Worcestershire sauce

- Tomato slices

- ¼ teaspoon dried thyme

- Onion Slices

- 1 teaspoon Tabasco sauce

- 4 slices of American cheese

- Mayonnaise

- 2 avocados

- Fresh Lettuce

- 4 sesame burger buns

- Pepper & salt to taste

Directions

1. Season the ground beef with Tabasco, Worcestershire sauce, thyme, pepper and salt. Lightly toss the ingredients using a fork until combined well. Make 4 palm sized beef patties from the mixture.

2. Prepare your grill pan over moderate heat. When done, place the beef patty over the pan & grill until you get your desired level of doneness, for 4 to 5 minutes per side. In the meantime; mash the avocado & season with pepper and salt. Add a small amount of spice, if desired.

3. When done, layer the bottom half of the bun with the mayonnaise, onion, lettuce and tomato. Add the hotbeef patty on top & then add on the cheese. Layer it with avocado & finally a few pieces of crispy bacon. Top it off with the top of the bun; serve immediately & enjoy.

Nutrition:

907 Calories

61g Total Fats

40g Protein

Chili's 1975 Soft Tacos

Preparation Time: 20 minutes

Cooking Time: 12 hours and 15 minutes

Servings: 6

Ingredients

- 1 ½ pounds beef chuck pot roast, fat trimmed

- 12 corn tortillas (6" each)

- 5 teaspoons chili powder

- 2 jars mild or medium tomato-based salsa (16 ounces each)

- 3 cups fresh lettuce, shredded

- 1 avocado

- 2 tablespoons cider vinegar

- ¾ cup sour cream

Directions

1. Spoon a cup of salsa into a small bowl & reserve. Combine the leftover salsa with chili powder and vinegar in a slow cooker. Add beef; cover & cook for 10 to 12 hours on low-heat, until the beef shreds easily. Shred the meat, using two forks & spoon into a large- sized serving bowl.

2. Preheat oven to 300 F. Stack the tortillas, wrap in foil & bake in the preheated oven for 8 to 10 minutes, until warm. Place lettuce and sour cream in bowls. Just before serving; pit, peel & dice the avocado & place in a small bowl. Put out the bowls (including the salsa) & assemble tacos at table.

Nutrition:

901 Calories

62g Total Fats

42g Protein

Spicy Shrimp Tacos

Preparation Time: 15 minutes

Cooking Time: 15 minutes

Servings: 2

Ingredients

- 6 to 8 shrimp peeled, de-veined, with tails off (3 to 4 per taco)
- 2 slices avocado
- 1/3 cup cabbage, finely shredded
- 2 flour tortillas, small
- 1 tablespoon Siracha
- 2 tablespoon mayonnaise
- ½ tablespoon Thai Sweet Chili Sauce
- 1-2 tablespoon olive oil
- A pinch each of chili powder, ground black pepper & salt

Directions

1. Wipe the surface of a grill pan with olive oil and heat it over medium-high heat. Season the shrimp with thechili powder, pepper and salt then grill until done, for 3 to 5 minutes.

2. Combine the mayo together with Siracha and sweet chili sauce in a small bowl.

3. Warm the tortillas & place half of the cabbage on each. Drizzle half of the sauce on each taco and then top with the shrimp. Serve immediately; garnished with the avocado & enjoy.

Nutrition:

911 Calories

63g Total Fats

39g Protein

Ranchero Chicken Tacos

Preparation Time: 15 minutes

Cooking Time: 15 minutes

Servings: 8

Ingredients

- Cheddar cheese, shredded
- Flour tortillas
- Chicken breast, slicedFor Ranchero Sauce
- 2 garlic cloves, chopped
- 1 Serrano or jalapeno chili, seeded & diced
- ¼ cup of chopped onion
- 3 cups tomatoes, diced
- ½ teaspoon ground chili
- 1 tablespoon oregano
- 2 tablespoons cooking oil

Directions

For Ranchero Sauce:

1. Over moderate heat in a large saucepan; heat the oil until hot & then sauté the onions, garlic and Serrano for a couple of minutes.

2. Decrease the heat & add in the tomatoes; stir well & cook until the tomatoes have wilted, for 5 to 6

minutes. Add the seasonings & let simmer for 5 minutes more.

For Quesadilla

1. Sauté or grill the chicken. Mix the chicken with the prepared sauce. Butter the outside of your tortilla. Add the chicken-ranchero sauce filling and cheese. Fold the tortilla & cook in a hot skillet.
2. Serve hot & enjoy.

Nutrition:

869 Calories

58g Total Fats

38g Protein

Beef Bacon Ranch Quesadillas

Preparation Time: 25 minutesCooking Time: 35 minutes Servings: 4

Ingredients

- 1 package cooked bacon, finely chopped
- Ranch dressing bottled
- 1 package Mexican cheese or cheddar, shredded
- 4 chicken breasts (baked or grilled), finely chopped
- 1-2 packages whole-grain or tortillas flour

Directions

1. While you are baking or grilling the chicken until completely cooked, brown the bacon in a large skillet until turn golden brown and cooked through; set aside at room temperature to cool.

2. Finely chop the chicken and bacon. Using low-fat cooking spray; lightly coat your heated griddle & place two tortillas down to brown. Lightly drizzle the ranch over the tortillas.

3. Sprinkle the chicken and bacon onto the ranch, top with the shredded cheese. Place a tortilla on top, smooch down with your hand to set it together, & carefully flip.

Once browned, pull them out from the heat and transfer them onto a large plate.

4. Once done, cut each one up into triangle sections using a super-sharp knife or pizza cutter, roughly eight triangles per tortilla.

Nutrition:

879 Calories

55g Total Fats

38g Protein

Chapter 3

Dressing Recipes

BKraft Thousand Island Dressing

Preparation Time: 5 minutes

Cooking Time: 0 minute

 Servings: 16

Ingredients

- 1 cup mayonnaise
- ¼ cup ketchup
- 2 tablespoons white vinegar
- 4 teaspoons white sugar
- 2 teaspoons sweet pickle relish, minced
- 2 teaspoons white onion, finely chopped or minced
- ¼ teaspoon sea salt
- ¼ teaspoon black pepper

Directions

1. Take a large bowl and combine all the ingredients in it.Mix well. Serve.

Nutrition:

67 Calories

4.9g Total Fats

6g Carbs

Newman Own's Creamy Caesar Salad Dressing

Preparation Time: 5 minutes

Cooking Time: 0 minute

Servings: 10

Ingredients

- 2 cups mayonnaise
- 6 tablespoons white vinegar, distilled
- ¼ cup Parmesan cheese, grated
- 4 teaspoons Worcestershire sauce
- 1 teaspoon lime juice
- 1 teaspoon dry mustard, ground
- 1/3 teaspoon salt, or to taste
- ½ teaspoon garlic powder
- ½ teaspoon onion powder
- ½ teaspoon black pepper, freshly ground
- 1 pinch basil, dried
- 1 pinch oregano, dried

Directions

1. Take an electric mixer and blend all the ingredients until smooth. Chill the prepared dressing for a few hours before severing. Enjoy.

Nutrition:

215 Calories

17.4g Total Fats

2.3g Protein

Bull's Eye Original BBQ Sauce

Preparation Time: 20 minutes

Cooking Time: 15 minutes

Servings: 4

Ingredients

- 1½ cups tomato ketchup
- ½ cup Worcestershire sauce
- 5 tablespoons butter, melted
- ¼ cup white vinegar
- 1 tablespoon yellow mustard
- ¼ cup onions, finely minced
- 2 tablespoons hickory liquid smoke
- ½ teaspoon Tabasco sauce
- 1 cup sugar, brown
- 1 tablespoon white sugar
- Salt, to taste

Directions

1. Incorporate ingredients in a saucepan and heat it over medium heat. Simmer the ingredients for 15 minutes, stirring occasionally. Put off the heat and let the sauce get cold. The sauce is ready.

Nutrition:

112 Calories

13.7 Total Fats

20.5g Carbs

Kraft Miracle Whip

Preparation Time: 20 minutes

Cooking Time: 15 minutes

Servings: 2

Ingredients

- 4 egg yolks
- 1/3 teaspoon salt
- 2 tablespoons powdered sugar
- 6 tablespoons lemon juice
- 2 cups oil
- 2 tablespoons cornstarch
- 2 teaspoons dry mustard
- 1 cup boiling water
- ¼ cup vinegar
- Table salt, to taste

Directions

1. Take a blender and add egg yolks along with salt, sugar, and half of lemon juice. Blend for few seconds until combined. While the blender is running, start adding the oil, a few drops at a time.

2. Add the remaining lemon juice. Turn off the blender. In a bowl, mix together cornstarch, water, mustard, and vinegar.

3. Mix until a smooth paste is formed. Pour the bowl ingredients into a pan. Cook on low heat until thickened. Slowly add this cooked mixture into the blender.

4. Turn on the blender and combine all the ingredients well. Transfer to a jar and let cool in the refrigerator.

Nutrition:

717 Calories

7.6g Total Fats

0.6 Carbs

Hellman's Mayonnaise

Preparation Time: 15 minutes

Cooking Time: 0 minute

Servings: 2

Ingredients

- 3 large egg yolks
- 1 teaspoon dry mustard
- 1 teaspoon salt
- ½ teaspoon cayenne pepper
- 1½ cups canola oil
- 4–6 tablespoons lemon juice

Directions

1. Add mustard and egg yolks into a blender and pulse until combined. While the blender is blending set the speed to low and start adding the oil very slowly.
2. Stop the blender and scrape down the mayonnaise. Add the lemon juice and remaining oil. Keep on blending until combined. At the end add salt and cayenne pepper. Mix and serve.

Nutrition:

362 Calories

39.1g Total Fats

3.4g Protein

Heinz Ketchup

Preparation Time: 25 minutes

Cooking Time: 20 minutes

Servings: 4

Ingredients

- 1 cup tomato paste
- 1/3 cup light corn syrup
- ½ cup white vinegar
- 1/3 cup water
- 2 tablespoons sugar
- Salt, to taste
- 1/3 teaspoon onion powder
- ¼ teaspoon garlic powder

Directions

1. Combine all the ingredients in a saucepan. Put on the heat and let the liquid simmer for 20 minutes. Put off the heat and let the mixture cool down. Store in airtight glass jar or serve with French fries.

Nutrition:

78 Calories

0.2 Total Fats

1.4g Protein

Mcdonald's Sabra Hummus

Preparation Time: 5 minutes

Cooking Time: 0 minute

Servings: 4

Ingredients

- 1 (14-ounce) can chickpeas, drained
- 1/3 cup tahini sauce
- Juice of 1 lemon
- 2 cloves garlic
- Salt and black pepper, to taste
- 1 teaspoon olive oil

Directions

1. With a high-speed blender to blend all the ingredients thoroughly. Serve and enjoy.

Nutrition:

576 Calories

27g Total Fats

24g Protein

Lawry's Taco Seasonings

Preparation Time: 10 minutes

Cooking Time: 0 minute

 Servings: 2

Ingredients

- 2 tablespoons flour
- 2 teaspoons red chili powder
- 2 teaspoons paprika
- 1½ teaspoons salt, or to taste
- 1½ teaspoons onion powder
- 1 teaspoon cumin
- ½ teaspoon cayenne pepper
- ½ teaspoon garlic powder
- ½ teaspoon white sugar
- ¼ teaspoon oregano, ground

Directions

Mix all the spices in a bowl and store in a glass jar.

Nutrition:

1 Calories

0.3g Total Fats

0.5g Protein

Mrs. Dash Salt-Free Seasoning Mix

Preparation Time: 5 minutes

Cooking Time: 0 minute

Servings: 2

Ingredients

- 2 teaspoons onion powder
- 2 teaspoons black pepper
- 2 teaspoons parsley
- 2 teaspoons dry celery seed
- 1 teaspoon dry basil
- 1 teaspoon dry bay leaf
- 2 teaspoons marjoram
- 2 teaspoons oregano
- 2 teaspoons savory
- 2 teaspoons thyme
- 2 teaspoons cayenne pepper
- 1 teaspoon coriander
- 2 teaspoons cumin
- 1 teaspoon mustard powder
- 2 teaspoons rosemary
- 2 teaspoons garlic powder
- 1 teaspoon mace

Directions

Mix all the spices in a bowl and store in a glass jar. Keepit dry.

Nutrition:

23 Calories

0.8g Total Fats

4g Carbs

0.9g Protein

Old Bay Seasoning by Peiwei's

Preparation Time: 4 minutes

Cooking Time: 0 minute

Servings: 4

Ingredients

- ¼ cup bay leaf powder
- ¼ cup celery salt
- 2 tablespoons dry mustard
- 4 teaspoons black pepper, ground
- 4 teaspoons ginger, ground
- 4 teaspoons paprika, smoked
- 2 teaspoons white pepper, ground
- 2 Teaspoons nutmeg, ground
- 2 teaspoons cloves, ground
- 2 teaspoons allspice, ground
- 1 teaspoon crushed red pepper flakes
- 1 teaspoon mace, ground
- 1 teaspoon cardamom, ground
- ½ teaspoon cinnamon, ground

Directions

1. Mix all the spices in a bowl and store in a glass jar. Keepit dry.

Nutrition:

16 Calories

0.7g Total Fats

0.6g Protein

Lawry's Seasoned Salt

Preparation Time: 5 minutes

Cooking Time: 0 minute

Serving: 1

Ingredients

- 1 tablespoon salt, or to taste
- 2 teaspoons white sugar
- ¼ teaspoon smoked paprika
- ¼ teaspoon turmeric powder
- ¼ teaspoon onion powder
- ¼ teaspoon garlic powder
- ¼ teaspoon cornstarch

Directions

Mix all the spices then store in a glass jar. Keep it dry.

Nutrition:

360 mg Sodium

97 Calories

18g Fats

Kraft Stove Top Stuffing Mix

Preparation Time: 5 minutes

Cooking Time: 10 minutes

Servings: 8

Ingredients

- 6 cups bread, cut into cubes

- 1 tablespoon parsley, flakes

- 3–4 bouillon cubes, chicken

- ¼ cup onion flakes, dried

- ½ cup celery flakes, dried

- 1 teaspoon thyme, dry

- 1 teaspoon black pepper

- ½ teaspoon sage

- ½ teaspoon salt

Directions

1. Preheat oven to 375°F. Bake the bread in the oven for 10 minutes. Once cool, dump all the ingredients in a bowl. Shake well to combine.

2. Tip: To use the prepared mixture, mix 2 cups mixture with ½ cup water and 2 tablespoons melted butter.

Nutrition:

57 Calories

0.7g Total Fats

2.9g Protein

Burger Sauce by Chili

Preparation Time: 5 minutes

Cooking Time: 0 minute

 Serving: 12

Ingredient

- 1 tbsp. gherkin

- ½ tsp. chopped dill

- ¾ tsp. onion powder

- ¾ tsp. garlic powder

- 1/8 tsp. ground white pepper

- ½ cup mayonnaise

- 1 tsp. mustard powder

- ½ tsp. erythritol sweetener

- ¼ tsp. sweet paprika

- 1 tsp. white vinegar

Direction

1. Using medium bowl, situate all the ingredients for the sauce in it then stir until well mixed.

2. Situate sauce for a minimum of overnight in the refrigerator to develop flavors and then serve with

burgers.

Nutrition:

15 Calories

7g Fats

2g Protein

Mcdonald's Caramel Sauce

Preparation Time: 5 minutes

Cooking Time: 15 minutes

 Serving: 12

Ingredient:

- 3 tablespoons erythritol sweetener

- 1 teaspoon vanilla extract, unsweetened

- 1/3 cup butter, salted

- 2/3 cup heavy cream

Direction:

1. With medium saucepan, situate it over low heat, mix in butter and erythritol and then cook for 4 minutes.
2. Mix in cream, bring it to a gentle boil then simmer the sauce for 10 minutes, stirring continuously.
3. Pull out pan from heat, stir in vanilla extract and thenserve.

Nutrition:

91 Calories

10g Fats

1g Protein

Paula Deen BBQ Sauce

Preparation Time: 5 minutes

Cooking Time: 5 minutes

Serving: 32

Ingredient:

- 1 tsp. onion powder

- 1 tsp. salt

- ½ tsp. cayenne pepper

- 1 tsp. ground black pepper

- ¾ cup erythritol sweetener

- 2 tsp. paprika

- ½ tsp. cinnamon

- 2 tbsp. mustard paste

- ½ tsp. xanthan gum

- 3 tbsp. lemon juice

- 1 ½ tbsp. liquid smoke

- ½ cup apple cider vinegar

- ¾ cup ketchup, low-carb

- ½ cup of water

- 1 tbsp. Worcestershire sauce

Direction:

1. Using medium saucepan, situate it over medium heat, mix mustard, Worcestershire sauce, liquid smoke, and ketchup in it, then pour in vinegar, lemon juice, and water.
2. Mix until combined, cook it for 3 to 4 minutes then whisk in xanthan gum until incorporated.
3. Stir in erythritol and all the spices, whisk until combined, and remove the pan from heat.
4. Allow the sauce cool completely, then serve immediately or store it in an air-tight jar or squeeze bottle.

Nutrition:

10 Calories

2g Fats

2g Carbs

Chorizo Queso Fundido

Preparation Time: 5 minutes

Cooking Time: 25 minutes

Serving: 6

Ingredient:

- 8 ounces Mexican chorizo

- 1 Roma tomato

- 2 tablespoons garlic

- 1/2 of a large onion

- 1 cup Mexican cream

- 1 roasted poblano pepper

- ½ teaspoon sea salt

- 2 cups Monterey Jack Cheese

Direction:

- Using big skillet pan, put it over medium heat, stir in chorizo, break it up then cook for 11 minutes.
1. Once done, drain excess grease, transfer chorizo to a bowl, and then set it aside.
2. Put pan over medium heat, mix in onion then cook it for 5 minutes.
3. Mix in tomato, pepper strips and garlic, season with salt, cook the mixture for 2 minutes then

scoop themixture into the bowl containing chorizo.

4. Pull away skillet pan from the heat, mix in cream and cheese, and then blend for 5 minutes or more.

5. Return the skillet pan at medium heat, add half of the chorizo mixture, stir and cook for 6 minutes.

6. Top it with the remaining chorizo mixture, situate the pan under the broiler and cook for 3 minutes.

7. Serve it with low-carb tortilla chips.

Nutrition:

402 Calories

33g Fats

22g Protein

Alfredo Sauce

Preparation Time: 5 minutes

Cooking Time: 10 minutes

 Serving: 6

Ingredient:

- 1 tablespoon minced garlic
- 1/8 teaspoon salt
- 1/8 teaspoon ground white pepper
- 1/8 teaspoon ground nutmeg
- 1 ½ cups grated Parmesan cheese
- 2 cups heavy whipping cream
- ½ cup butter, unsalted
- 2 ounces cream cheese, softened

Direction:

1. Take a medium saucepan, place it over medium heat, add butter and when it melts, add garlic and then cook for 2 minutes until fragrant.
2. Then add cream cheese and heavy cream, stir until just mixed and stir in parmesan until melted.
3. Cook the sauce for 5 to 7 minutes until sauce thickens to the desired level and then stir in salt, white pepper, and nutmeg. Serve straight away.

Nutrition:

531 Calories

53.8g Fats

10.3g Protein

Don Pablo's Prairie Fire Bean Dip

Preparation Time: 10minutes

Cooking Time: 15 minutes

Servings: 6

Ingredients

- 1 tablespoon oil

- ½ cup finely chopped onion

- 1 (15-ounce) can fava or pinto beans

- 2 tablespoons plain yogurt

- 2 chipotle chilis, finely chopped

- 1 tablespoon adobo sauce from the chilis

- 1 jalapeño pepper, diced

- 1 teaspoon salt

- ½ teaspoon garlic powder

- ½ teaspoon cumin

- ½ cup shredded cheddar or Monterey Jack cheese

- Additional cheese and jalapeños for topping, if desired

- Chips or soft flour tortillas cut into quarters (for serving)

Directions

1. In a medium skillet, warm the oil over medium heatand add the onion. Cook until softened. Strain the beans and stir in the skillet. Mix in the yogurt, chilies, adobo sauce, jalapeño, salt, garlic powder, and cumin. Cook to heat through.

2. Transfer the dip to a blender and pulse until smooth. (You can leave some chunks if you like.) Transfer the dip to a heatproof serving dish and stir in the cheese. Serve warm, garnished with additional cheese and jalapeños if desired.

Nutrition:

706 Calories

50g Total Fats

35g Protein

Café Rio's Pico de Gallo

Preparation Time: 5 minutes

Cooking Time: 0 minute

Servings: 6

Ingredients

- 5 ripe tomatoes, finely diced

- ½ teaspoon salt

- 1 medium sweet onion, finely diced

- 4 cloves garlic, minced

- 1 bunch cilantro, finely chopped

- 1–2 jalapeño peppers, seeded and diced

- 1 tablespoon lime juice

- 4 shakes green Tabasco sauce

Directions

1. Mix all the ingredients. Serve at room temperature.

Nutrition:

664 Calories

48g Total Fats

29g Protein

Chipotle's Refried Beans

Preparation Time: 5 minutes

Cooking Time: 2 ½ hours

Servings: 6

Ingredients

- 1-pound dried pinto beans

- 6 cups warm water

- ½ cup bacon fat

- 2 teaspoons salt

- 1 teaspoon cumin

- ½ teaspoon black pepper

- ½ teaspoon cayenne pepper

Directions

1. Rinse and drain the pinto beans. Check them over and remove any stones. Transfer the beans in a Dutch oven and stir in the water. Bring the pot to a boil, reduce the heat, and simmer for 2 hours, stirring frequently.

2. When the beans are tender, reserve ½ cup of the boiling water and drain the rest. Heat the bacon fat in a large, deep skillet. Add the beans 1 cup at a

time, mashing and stirring as you go. Add the spices and some of the cooking liquid if the beans are too dry.

Nutrition:

661 Calories

49g Total Fats

28g Protein

Abuelo's Jalapeño Cheese Fritters

Preparation Time: 15 minutes

Cooking Time: 20 minutes

 Servings: 8

Ingredients

- Fritters

- 1 (8-ounce) package cream cheese, softened

- ½ cup Monterrey cheese, shredded

- ½ cup cheddar cheese, shredded

- 3 jalapeños, deseeded and finely chopped

- 1 teaspoon Lawry's seasoning

- Oil for frying

- Breading

- 3 cups breadcrumbs

- ¼ cup all-purpose flour

- Egg Wash

- 2 eggs

- ¼ cup water

Directions

Grease and preheat at 300 degrees. Blend all the ingredients then form the mixture into 1-inch balls makes approximately 20 balls). Place onto the prepared sheet and set aside.

1. Beat the eggs and water together until slightly frothy; set aside. To two separate bowls, add the flour and breadcrumbs; set aside.

2. Assembling

3. Roll the balls in the flour first. Dunk each ball into the egg wash and then into the breadcrumbs. Toss until evenly coated. Cook the oil at 350°F and fry the balls until evenly golden brown. Drain the balls on a paper towel. Serve with your favorite dip.

Nutrition:

636 Calories

47g Total Fats

30g Protein

Chipotle's Guacamole

Preparation Time: 10 minutes

Cooking Time: 0 minutes

 Serving: 6

Ingredients

- 1 medium jalapeño pepper, seeded and deveined, finelychopped
- 1 cup diced red onion
- 2 tablespoons fresh cilantro, chopped finely
- 8 ripe avocados
- 8 teaspoons freshly squeezed lime juice
- 1 teaspoon kosher salt

Directions

1. Chop avocado in half and take out the flesh. Mix in the jalapeño pepper, onion, and cilantro. Drizzle the lime juice. Season it with salt. Pound avocado with the rest of the ingredients until desired consistency is achieved. Seal it with plastic wrap before serving.

Nutrition:

674 Calories

37g Total Fats

26g Protein

Chipotle's Queso Dip

Preparation Time: 15 minutes

Cooking Time: 2 hours

Servings: 8

Ingredients

- 1 cup cheddar, cubed

- 1 cup American cheese, cubed

- 1 cup Monterey Jack, cubed

- 1 cup heavy cream

- 2 poblano peppers

- 1 large Roma tomato, halved

- 1 teaspoon paprika

- 1 teaspoon garlic powder

- ¼ teaspoon cayenne pepper

- ½ teaspoon black pepper

- 1 tablespoon olive oil

- Tortilla chips to serve

Directions

Grease the baking dish with oil and preheat at 400 degrees. Place the tomatoes and poblano pepper in the prepared baking dish and bake until the skins are blackened.

1. Although the veggies are in the oven, mix remaining ingredients in a pot and let simmer on low. Once cooked, set aside and let cool at room temperature for about 10 minutes.
2. Remove the skins and transfer to a blender. Blend until pureed. Add the pureed veggies to the cheese mixture; mix well and continue cooking for 2 hours. Serve hot with tortilla chips.

Nutrition:

677 Calories

41g Total Fats

30g Protein

Chili's Original Chili

Preparation Time: 15 minutes

Cooking Time: 1 hour 30 minutes

Servings: 4

Ingredients

- Spice Blend

- ½ cup chili powder

- 1/8 cup salt

- 1/8 cup ground cumin

- 1 tablespoon paprika

- 1 teaspoon ground black pepper

- 1 teaspoon garlic powder

- 1 teaspoon of cayenne pepper

- Chili

- 4 pounds chuck, ground for chili

- 3¼ cups water

- 16 ounces tomato sauce

- 1½ cups yellow onions, chopped

- 1 tablespoon cooking oil

- Masa Harina

- 1 cup water

- 1 tablespoon masa harina

- Sliced green onions for garnish, if desired

Directions

1. Put all the spice blend ingredients in a bowl. Mix thoroughly and set the bowl aside. Cook the meat at medium heat in a stock pot until it is brown. While the meat is cooking, thoroughly mix together the spice mix, water, and tomato sauce.

2. Stir in spice mixture to the browned meat and bring to aboil. When chili is about to boil, sauté the onions in oil over medium heat for the meantime. When the chili is boiling and the onions are translucent, add the onions to the chili and stir.

3. Set heat to low and let the chili to simmer for an hour, stirring the mixture every 15 minutes. In a bowl, mix the masa harina ingredients together. When the chili has been cooking for an hour, add the masa harina mixture to the chili and cook for another 10 minutes.

4. Transfer the chili to a bowl, garnish green onions, if desired, and serve.

Nutrition:

681 Calories

48g Total Fats

32g Protein

Ingredient Tahini Paste

Preparation Time: 15 minutes

Cooking Time: 30 minutes

 Servings: 16

Ingredients:

- 1 cup of hulled sesame seeds

- 3 tbsps. extra virgin olive oil

Directions:

1. Pour the sesame seeds into a pan and roast over medium-high heat, stirring regularly, until the seeds are brown.

2. Let seeds to cool then situate them in a blender/food processor. Drizzle in 3 tbsps of olive oil and process until a paste is formed. Slowly add in more oil until you reach the consistency you'd prefer.

3. Thoroughly stir the paste before storing the tahini in an airtight jar/container and place in the refrigerator. Tahini can be stored for about 3 months.

Nutrition:

36 Calories

76 Fats

1g Protein

Spicy Mexican Barbecue Sauce

Preparation Time: 15 minutes

Cooking Time: 15 minutes

Servings: 12

Ingredients:

- 2/3 olive oil

- 1 onion, diced

- ½ tbsp garlic paste

- 1 ½ tsps. of salt

- 1 chili pepper, seeded & diced

- 2 tomatoes, peeled & chopped

- 2 tbsps. of chili powder

- 2 tbsps. of sugar

- ¼ cup of vinegar

- ¼ cup of beer

Directions:

1. Cook oil in a pan over medium heat. Drop in the onions and fry until browned.
2. Stir in the garlic, chili, chili powder, salt and tomatoes. Simmer for 4 minutes

3. Pour in the sugar, vinegar and beer and let it simmer for 10 minutes, stirring regularly. Remove from heat and let it cool.

Nutrition:

126 Calories

11.6g Fats

0.7g Protein

Tangy French Remoulade Sauce

Preparation Time: 15 minutes

Cooking Time: 15 minutes

Servings: 8

Ingredients:

- ¾ cup of mayonnaise

- 1 ½ tbsp of cornichon or dill relish

- 1 tsp of finely chopped capers

- 1 tbsp of lemon juice

- 1 tbsp of mustard (preferably Dijon)

- 2 tsp of chopped parsley

- 1 dash of hot sauce

- ½ tsp of salt

Direction:

1. Incorporate mayonnaise with the cornichon, capers, lemon juice, mustard, salt and parsley together. Stir in the hot sauce and then cover with plastic wrap. Place in the refrigerator until needed.

Nutrition:

146 Calories

1g Carbs

16g Fat

Conclusion

Everyone has some dishes they like the most, and others love to have a bite of their favorite recipes at home. Will you be the first to make a copycat recipe that tastes the same as the original one? Or will you mix in the wrong ingredients and damage the recipe so that you end up with a concoction that tastes weird?

You need to have all your ingredients collected, mix them up, and see how you can make the taste just like the original recipe.

Following a few simple tips and tricks, you can make quality cuisine in your kitchen. These tricks may not seem so strong on their own but can transform how you prepare food when they are all used together.

The major advantage of trying copycat restaurant recipes is that you can save more money and use your creativity to improve the dishes. You can also adjust the ingredients and add those favorite herbs to your desired taste. You may not include some ingredients of your favorite dish when you try the copycat recipes, and it is okay.

It is not hard to acquire those top-secret restaurant-quality recipes. Others may advise that you need to have culinary credentials to cook those secret recipes. Yet, we can gather those ingredients ourselves and cook an elaborate meal that tastes like the real deal.

But do top secret restaurant recipes taste the way the chef served them? Perhaps. You can easily recreate your favorite recipes with patience and a little practice. You may start to think that some recipes need additional seasonings to improve your dish than the original. Nevertheless, if you wanted to prepare this dish on your own, there is still a chance.